YOUR KNOWLEDGE HAS VALUE

- We will publish your bachelor's and master's thesis, essays and papers

- Your own eBook and book - sold worldwide in all relevant shops

- Earn money with each sale

Upload your text at www.GRIN.com and publish for free

Bibliographic information published by the German National Library:

The German National Library lists this publication in the National Bibliography; detailed bibliographic data are available on the Internet at http://dnb.dnb.de .

This book is copyright material and must not be copied, reproduced, transferred, distributed, leased, licensed or publicly performed or used in any way except as specifically permitted in writing by the publishers, as allowed under the terms and conditions under which it was purchased or as strictly permitted by applicable copyright law. Any unauthorized distribution or use of this text may be a direct infringement of the author s and publisher s rights and those responsible may be liable in law accordingly.

Imprint:

Copyright © 2016 GRIN Verlag, Open Publishing GmbH
Print and binding: Books on Demand GmbH, Norderstedt Germany
ISBN: 9783668275454

This book at GRIN:

http://www.grin.com/en/e-book/337638/joothan-a-dalit-s-life-by-omprakash-valmiki-a-book-review

Pratyusha Guha

"Joothan: A Dalit's Life" by Omprakash Valmiki. A Book Review

GRIN Publishing

GRIN - Your knowledge has value

Since its foundation in 1998, GRIN has specialized in publishing academic texts by students, college teachers and other academics as e-book and printed book. The website www.grin.com is an ideal platform for presenting term papers, final papers, scientific essays, dissertations and specialist books.

Visit us on the internet:

http://www.grin.com/

http://www.facebook.com/grincom

http://www.twitter.com/grin_com

BOOK REVIEW: 'JOOTHAN', BY OMPRAKASH VALMIKI

PAPER XIV HIST0601: Social Identities and Movements in Colonial and Post colonial South Asia

INTRODUCTION

After the independence of India, the political leaders of our nation had attempted to eradicate the ominous practice of untouchability through various sanctions in government laws and policies, the validation of its dismantled state was further cemented by the Constitution of India which came into power in 1950. However the scope of removal of untouchability remained limited only to be put pen to paper. That is to say, legal changes were made within political framework, but mindsets of larger population were infected with germ of obnoxious caste system. Caste system of India has allotted the untouchables to lowest echelon of society. This segregated class of people has remained downtrodden and is forbidden by the so called upper castes of society to climb up the social ladder and settle themselves down at a better place in society. Labelling them as the depressed class, scheduled class by constitution or addressing them as Harijans by Gandhi failed to confine the anguished state of mind of those people caused by the abhorrence meted out to them by their own fellow countrymen and women. The dubious and tumultuous nature of their realistic lives and experiences could not be made non-visible by wrapping the facts under the garb of law and administration, hopes and aspirations bestowed upon the ex-untouchables by the national leaders. The multifarious trajectories undertaken to comprehend and restrain the phenomenon of untouchability have still not dealt with the real life bizarre caste rigidity practices which promote exactly the opposite of the values what our state and its constitution strive to stand by. The identity crisis resurfaces with a thrust along the lines of precariousness.

The untouchables embraced the term "Dalit" first coined by Jyotirao Phule and further popularised by Dr. B. R. Ambedkar. Dalit signified the broken people, the defeated people. However, if read between the lines, it would be easier to perceive that the brokenness of people carried a silver lining of forging new self made identities emerged from the struggles and every kind of impediment encountered in their treads of progression. To convey their unheard words, unfelt emotions, above all, rectify the misconstrued facts of their lives, the Dalits, who have been fortunate enough to cultivate knowledge and scholarship and secured alleged high esteemed disposition in society, have articulated such reminiscence and disseminated them through the medium of cultural, literary events, popularly and collectively known as Dalit literature.

DALIT AUTOBIOGRAPHY AND 'JOOTHAN'

Dalit autobiographies act as distinctive part of Dalit literature. The nature of autobiographies is transparent and inclusive. Autobiographies present the real life experiences, but it goes beyond the life of the writer. Not only does Dalit autobiography speak about life of an individual plagued with the oppression of caste system but it speaks at communal level. Story of one Dalit life provides an insight to the lives of many other Dalit people. Though one autobiographical character remains the locus, the stories of supporting characters are also significant to be paid heed to. One such Dalit autobiography is 'Joothan', written by Omprakash Valmiki. The autobiography was written in Hindi, later its translation in English by Arun Prabha Mukherjee secured for it a national recognition by expanding the scope of readership.

Joothan is a collection of memoirs. The nature of non linearity of the story precludes the monotony to take a heavy toll on the minds of readers. It is rather a dovetail sewed with the author's fragment memories of his childhood filled with hardships pertaining to his belonging in the 'Chuhra' community. Throughout the text, Valmiki makes it a point to assert the undeniable differences between the untouchables and the upper caste people, which had already been created by the caste hierarchization of society. He is extremely polemical in reacting to hypocrisy of Gandhiji to call the untouchables the children of God and at the same time to urge for preservation of Varna system of Indian society. To Valmiki, 'The pigs wandering in narrow lanes, naked children, dogs, daily fights this was the environment of my childhood. If the people who call the caste system an ideal social arrangement had to live in this environment for a day or two, they would change their mind'. Thus, implication of his statement is to make an urge to the loquacious bunch of upper caste people to step into the shoes of a Dalit to feel the bitterness of this hellish life, which can be otherwise, only be experienced by Dalit himself. Also, in many other instances, Valmiki elaborates the distinguishing idiosyncrasies of lives of Dalits than that of upper caste 'Tyagis' of their village. He points out the 'the deities worshipped by the Dalits are 'different from Hindu deities and their names won't be found in any 'Purana' even if one searches hard' and also Dalits worship 'Jaharpir' at 'Janmashtami' and 'Mai Madaran' during 'Deepawali' in lieu of Lord Krishna and goddess 'Lakshmi' respectively. I perceive this assertion of differences in voice of Valmiki as an attempt on the part of his community to stand out of the Hindu fold, to prohibit itself from being a part of socio-religious integrated system of Hinduism. The scrupulous mention of the dichotomy between Dalits as 'we', 'us' and upper castes as 'they', 'them' is significantly manifested throughout his text. The subhuman existence of Chuhra community, its plight of everyday and groaning of hunger and starvation, deprivation of reverent existence, are all encapsulated in the term "Joothan". Valmiki narrates for us the values of joothan or leftover received by them from the Tyagi upper caste community. The leftover foods were rugged and grubby in nature, albeit the Chuhra's had them with relish. The consumption of pork by the 'Chuhras' were looked down upon by the 'Tyagis', the author also notes that 'The behaviour of (this) Muslim Tagas was just like that of the Hindu Tagas'. On being exasperated at the general rebuking character of upper castes people, Hindu and Muslim Tyagis both alike, Valmiki at one instance bewrayed their hypocrite temperament and he went on to say 'At such moments I would think of all the Tyagis who came in the darkness of the night to the Bhangi basti to eat pork. ..Those who came to eat meat secretly at night in day light observed untouchability in front of everybody.'

The author's struggle to adjust to the educational ambience of school, primarily marked by the presence of upper castes Tyagis was burdensome and exhausting. The fact that, so called untouchables getting an opportunity of receiving education meant forging of arduous parity between the upper castes Tyagis and the ex-untouchables 'Chuhra' which was frowned upon by the former community. Thus the untouchables became easy targets of the wrath of Tyagis. Valmiki expressed through penning down his story his helplessness when people teased him by calling "Chuhre ke", credential was his determination which got him through this nauseating phase and made him what he was in his later life. The caste discrimination had expanded from his dwelling to the school, so expanded the range of animosity to the author. He was isolated and made sit on a corner of the room. His other friends who were too untouchables, Ram Singh and Sukkham Singh were treated alike. Valmiki narrates an incident of unspeakable torture of Sukkham Singh by Kaliram, the headmaster of their school. Kaliram also compelled young Valmiki to sweep the entire school premises. Despite all the hurdles on his way, the author endured hardships in the hope that his father's words might come true, that was to improve caste by education. Never indulgent in menial works, Omprakash found it disgraceful to scavenging, reaping and disposing dead cattle. The conviction of improving caste by learning and education which was transferred from his father to the author tormented the already restless mind of Valmiki when he was asked to perform the ancestral function of reaping and disposing of cattle. He felt a trance of falling into the pit of wretchedness of untouchability, which the author was trying to escape incessantly.

Omprakash's family performed the menial jobs for the Tyagis, for which no wages or negligible wages were paid to them, but for most of the cases the untouchable counted on the Joothans or the scraps in return of their service. Valmiki narrates an incident when his mother discarded the Joothan due to the humiliation meted out to her and her children. He recalls how the spirit of Mother Goddess had endowed on his mother, and translated the conventional attitude of pain and endurance to demeanour of protest or resistance. However, the point was these kinds of resistances were handful and finally succumbed to the age old dominance of the upper castes. Such was the case of Valmiki's mother, and I consider it as the blip of moment which elicited her scornful reaction, had the voices of resistances combined and agitated then the atrocities from the upper castes would have mellowed down to an extent. A proposition of this kind would not be just applicable to the context of 'Tyagi' and the 'Chuhra', but united voices of every dalit could have changed the general practice of strained relationship with the higher social order groups. Regrettably their extreme exclusion from social, religious, economical and political spheres by the so-called upper caste, precluded the untouchables or dalits from developing their individual rational consciousness, a volatile situation emerging out of it made them dependent on influential personalities for being represented rather than representing themselves.

The profound realization which dawned on Omprakash Valmiki was that caste could not be traversed, not even with the aid of education. Valmiki unmasks the so-called educated urban middle class peoples' attitude to the untouchables. His love-affair with Savita Kulkarni who hailed from a Maharashtrian Brahmin family got throttled just for his caste. He mentions a large number of urban educated people who were in some way or the other 'unhappy' with his surname. He reminds the callousness of Mr. Gupta, training in-charge at Jabalpur. He cites how his 'caste' soiled the normalcy in relationship with so many people like Deshpande in Ambernath, Dr. Naidu, Head of the Hindi Department at Nagpur University, Dr. Sukhvir Singh, Reader in Delhi University's Shivaji college, Harikishan Santoshi and Sardar Gyan Singh. Many of them advised him to change his surname to suppress his caste. Valmiki recognises this as 'a terrible crisis of identity' among educated Dalits. He is frowned upon by almost every educated upper caste individual he has encountered in his life because of his caste orientation. The very individuality of the author was deliberately overlooked and his identity was stereotypically entwined with his caste belonging, tending to nullify the fact that, a human being and his identity was much more worth than the caste from which he belonged. Omprakash Valmiki must be one of those lakhs who go through the same difficulty of proving their competency and being acknowledged by their society. The identity crisis issue is sickly prevalent and rampant in growth still today.

CONCLUSION

In this writing, I have analysed the current state of Dalits or the ex-untouchables in our society through the illustrated book review of Joothan. Firstly, the Dalit autobiographies are vital offshoot of Dalit literature, they are informative, imperative for us to examine the true functioning of social system characterised by the caste hierarchization embedded in it. These autobiographies and the stories shift attention of the readers from hypocritical sentiments and exaggerations enclosed in writings presented by the upper caste learned men to the stories based on lives, truths and actual grievances of people who went through all of it. In sum, from a critical point of view, the manipulation of facts and events are allegedly less expected to be inscribed in an autobiography written by a Dalit himself, than in any other form of written record. As far as the co-relation between the present state of Dalits in our India and the book Joothan is concerned, the delusion of egalitarianism, being imparted to every citizen of the society, irrespective of caste, class, religion is prominent and most importantly deceiving in practice. The social exclusion of an ex-untouchable is so overpowering that even though he attains economic and political mobility or even beyond the national boundaries through his hard labour, he is not accepted by the castes located higher up in the caste hierarchy as an equal. His social identity remains stigmatized and his achievements are basically associated with that social identity. It is high time we question the government and its institutions to put the theory of law into practice and take required steps to curtail down the hatred, disgusts amongst people to ensure healthy co-existence and growth of every kind of person in our society.

YOUR KNOWLEDGE HAS VALUE

- We will publish your bachelor's and master's thesis, essays and papers

- Your own eBook and book - sold worldwide in all relevant shops

- Earn money with each sale

Upload your text at www.GRIN.com
and publish for free